21 May – 20 June

amber
BOOKS

ASTROLOGICAL SIGN DATES:
The precise start and end times for each sign vary by a day or two from year to year as the Gregorian calendar shifts relative to the tropical year. The dates provided in this book are correct for the year 2020.

If you are unsure of the Zodiac sign for your specific birth year, visit: www.yourzodiacsign.com.

Gemini

21 May – 20 June

A guide to understanding yourself, your friendships and finding your true love

This edition first published in 2020 by
Amber Books Ltd
United House
North Road
London N7 9DP
United Kingdom
www.amberbooks.co.uk
Instagram: amberbooksltd
Facebook: amberbooks
Twitter: @amberbooks

ISBN: 978-1-83886-026-4

Project Editor: Sarah Uttridge
Design: Zoë Mellors

Picture Credits:
All illustrations by Fabbri Publications except the following:
Shutterstock: 32 (Elena Naumchenkova), 33 (La Puma), 35 (Slonomysh), 36 (Angel Soler Gollonet)

Printed and bound in China

TRADITIONAL CHINESE BOOKBINDING
This book has been produced using traditional Chinese bookbinding techniques, using a method that was developed during the Ming Dynasty (1368–1644) and remained in use until the adoption of Western binding techniques in the early 1900s. In traditional Chinese binding, single sheets of paper are printed on one side only, and each sheet is folded in half, with the printed pages on the outside. The book block is then sandwiched between two boards and sewn together through punched holes close to the cut edges of the folded sheets.

Contents

Introduction

Gemini

21 May–20 June

Sign: The Twins

Ruling Planet: Mercury

Gender: Masculine

Element: Air

Quality: Mutable

Compatibility: Aquarius

Non-compatibility: Taurus, Capricorn and Virgo

Every man, woman and child is born with a distinct and different destiny. There are no exceptions. Everyone has cosmic significance and a part to play in the life of the universe. This is innate and inescapable, and goes beyond the tiny boundaries of nation, creed and colour.

As we live out our lives on planet Earth, we are, however unknowingly, acting in a greater drama and reacting to impulses that come from distant astronomical bodies, stars and planets millions of light years away. Sceptics pour scorn on the idea that far-distant Saturn, for example, can have any effect on our lives, as the ancient art and science of astrology teaches. But the fact is that we are sparks of energy inhabiting bodies made of the same stuff as the stars, responding like tiny radios to the distant messages they send to Earth.

Each infant carries within it a double blueprint for life: its genetic programming and the pattern of character that comes from the astrological 'clock' that was set in motion at the moment of birth. No one knows the full extent of genetic influence, although it seems to be astonishingly far-reaching, but the power of the horoscope has been well known to the wisest men and women for many centuries.

Our Sun signs provide essential inside information about our destinies. They reveal the secrets of who we really are, and why we are here, laying out before us our potential, the sort of joys and achievements our characteristics may bring about, and warn us of problems to be overcome through the triumph of free will.

Read this book with an open mind and discover who you really are.

The Elements

Up to the beginning of the Age of Enlightenment – the modern scientific era – in the 18th century, it was commonly believed that everything, including human beings, was made up of the four elements: Earth, Air, Fire and Water. These were thought of as the building blocks of life, and each astrological sign had a predominance of one or another. Each created its common characteristics, although too much of any of the elements can produce an unbalanced personality.

Air Signs

The Air signs are Gemini, Libra and Aquarius. These inspirational, communicative signs of the zodiac can talk a lot of 'hot air', and their ability to cause a 'wind of change' to run through society is a mixed blessing.

This tendency is viewed with horror by the Earth signs, to whom all chance is fraught with danger. Often the Air signs are blown this way and that by sudden enthusiasms and conflicting, contradictory opinions, but they can throw new light on apparently intractable problems. It is their influence that helps sweep away outmoded ways of doing things, bringing in all manner of brave new worlds. Geminians talk and act fast, and live life at a furious pace, often doing several things at once – one of which is forever talking on the telephone. Librans are more cool and collected, the arbiters and diplomats of the zodiac, but they can be great ditherers, prone to sudden reversals of opinion.

Aquarians, the idealists and New Agers of the zodiac, can move swiftly if their crusading zeal is fully engaged, and their motivation is razor-sharp. If they feel something is best for humankind, they will go for it, dropping everything else, including all thoughts of personal comfort or gain. However, they can also be irritatingly nebulous and 'airy-fairy', often lost in their dreams of creating a brave new world while failing to make their mark on this one.

Air Signs
Gemini
Libra
Aquarius

Colours of the Zodiac

Traditionally, each sign of the zodiac has its own colour, which is believed to be 'lucky' or magically empowered for those born under that particular sign. In general, the colours are associated with the ruling planets and are symbolic of their attributes. Many people find that they feel most comfortable when wearing their sign's colours, and often choose them without knowing their full astrological background.

Gemini

Ruling Planet: Mercury.

Colour: Yellow or gold. This is the colour of speedy communication and of healing. It is energetic without being confrontational (like red) and is also the colour of optimism and of 'sunny' temperaments. Too much yellow, however, can discourage realistic long-term planning.

The Angelic Hierarchy

According to ancient tradition, each planet is governed by one of the great archangels, who are also rulers of certain aspects of human life. The box below lists the planet that they rule, the areas over which they have influence and their special day of the week.

Raphael

Archangel of Mercury.

Governs: Gemini and Virgo.

Rules: Writing and all forms of communication and learning as well as healing.

Day: Wednesday

The Genders

Traditionally, the twelve signs of the zodiac are divided into Masculine and Feminine, although of course both men and women are born into each.

The characteristics were assigned to the genders aeons ago, well before modern feminism or political correctness, and may now seem old-fashioned to many. However, the signs do seem to be grouped according to the appropriate gender.

The Masculine Signs

The Masculine signs are Aries, Gemini, Leo, Libra, Sagittarius and Aquarius. Masculine traits do tend to be accentuated in the Fire signs, which are Aries, Leo and Sagittarius.

Masculine signs are dominant and assertive, often to the point of being pugnacious and extroverted. They are natural leaders and rulers, showing fiery initiative and are fiercely protective of others in their care. They are pioneers and visionaries, conquerors of new lands and the first to achieve great things. They tend to tackle things themselves and can be impatient with others who are less assertive.

Negatively, Masculine signs can be egotistical, arrogant and cruel, and dismissive of the needs and feelings of others. They may turn out to be trouble-makers and rebels – violent, belligerent and inclined to subversion.

The Ruling Planets

Until the 18th century, astrologers knew only the planets of our solar system that could be seen with the naked eye: Mercury, Venus, Mars, Jupiter and Saturn. (For the purposes of astrology, the Sun and the Moon are also counted as planets even though the Sun is a star and the Moon is the satellite of Earth.) Uranus was discovered in 1781, Neptune in 1846 and Pluto was first seen in 1930. Many astrologers believe that the existence of other heavenly bodies – such as the rumoured Vulcan, which hypothetically exists within the orbit of Mercury – is about to be confirmed. Astrologers will then have to agree which signs these 'new' planets will rule, and what human characteristics their discovery will accentuate.

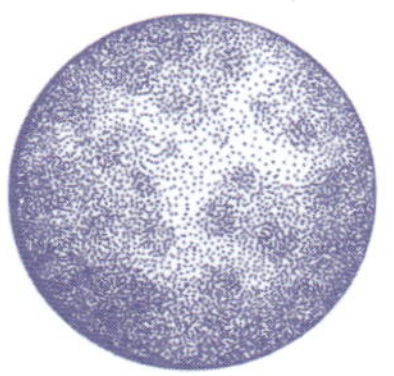

Mercury

Mercury was the name of the Roman messenger god, ruler of communication, whose great energy always kept him on the move. To help him travel fast he had little wings on his ankles and helmet. In Greek mythology he was Hermes, who gave his name to the legendary body of learning known as the Hermetica, which inspired thousands of great names over the centuries, from Leonardo da Vinci to Sir Isaac Newton. Although many scholars once believed that Hermeticism originated with the Greeks, there is increasing evidence that they had merely adapted much older Egyptian wisdom.

The Egyptian version of Mercury was Thoth, god of wisdom, healing and time. Known as 'Thrice-great Thoth', he was worshipped in the form of an ibis-headed man. His secrets were jealously guarded in temples specially dedicated to him in ancient Heliopolis, and passed on only to initiates who had proved worthy of them.

About Mercury

This tiny planet, the nearest to the Sun, is just 4880 km (3000 miles) across, with a year of 88 days – the second-fastest-moving heavenly body after the Moon.

The sacred day of Mercury is Wednesday.

In Scandinavia, the messenger god Loki was also a trickster. So was the Native American Heyeohkah, the mocking version of the creator god, who, nevertheless, showed kindness and compassion to humankind. All the mercurial gods share the same dual nature. They are both trickster and friend of the human race.

Mercury gave his name to quicksilver, the beautiful and unusual liquid metal, which – being a cumulative poison – is also deadly. Mercury proved to be of enduring fascination to generations of alchemists, who sought for centuries to turn this base metal into gold.

Gemini and Virgo are both ruled by Mercury. Typical Geminians are truly mercurial – quick-witted, fast talkers, energetic and volatile. However, there can also be an element of the trickster in them.

Virgoans are great communicators but at a slower pace than Gemini. They think before they speak and can be immensely entertaining, with a highly developed – often self-deprecating – sense of humour.

The modern era, with its unprecedented advances in communication – from the transmission of the first radio signals to the internet – has been an archetypically Mercurial epoch.

The Qualities

In addition to the influence of gender, the elements and the planets, each sign of the zodiac is affected by having an intrinsic quality – Cardinal, Fixed or Mutable.

Mutable Quality

Those born under the Mutable signs are always on the move, either physically or mentally, forever seeking fresh fields and pastures new. They are restless, versatile and flexible, hating routine and any form of strict discipline. These individuals can have butterfly minds, endlessly alighting on new enthusiasms, fads or crazes, then dropping them just as quickly and moving on to the next thing. Mutable people can be unreliable and irresponsible, and are rarely self-disciplined, although they are often extremely charming.

Gemini

Creative and persuasive, Geminians personify Mutable qualities. They loathe restriction of any kind and tend to despise more solid citizens. Forever seizing on the main chance, they are quick-witted and articulate, and can be very amusing. Extremely gregarious, they are unhappy alone or in the same unchanging environment. They often lack depth.

Signs and Symbols

Most people are familiar with the zodiac 'zoo' – the collection of symbols that represent the twelve signs. These images reflect the characteristics traditionally assigned to each sign and contain a wealth of knowledge about its true nature.

Each sign of the zodiac is represented by a symbol – the twin fish for Pisces, for example. No one is sure exactly when or why the symbols were chosen, although some authorities believe they date from Sumeria or Mesopotamia, 4000 years before Jesus Christ. The priest-astrologers of the ancient world were the first to impose recognizable patterns on the great constellations – Leo the Lion being one example.

Today, seeing such shapes in the stars may seem fanciful, but thousands of years ago imaginations were more poetic, and many myths told of magical animals, such as the dragon, which had strange powers to influence everyday human life.

Although the ancient Egyptians left few astrological records, they were almost unique in antiquity for worshipping archetypal, animal-headed gods. However, these strange hybrid gods – half-human, half-animal – were worshipped as aspects of one God. Contrary to the general belief that the Egyptians were idolaters, their religion was basically monotheistic. Each statue represented an aspect of the one true God.

Since they were established, the signs have remained unchanged, although there was a movement in the Middle Ages to change the sign of Aquarius into the sign of John the Baptist – presumably because of the connection with water.

The twelve signs of the Zodiac do seem particularly apt on the whole, and accurately reflect the archetypal character of typical Sun sign types. The great Swiss psychoanalyst Carl Gustav Jung (1875–1961) believed that, deep in our psyches, humanity shares a collective unconscious – a set of archetypal images, which, at a profound level, we all understand. The signs of the zodiac form part of this pool of images, conveying eternal truths to our unconscious minds.

Signs and Symbols

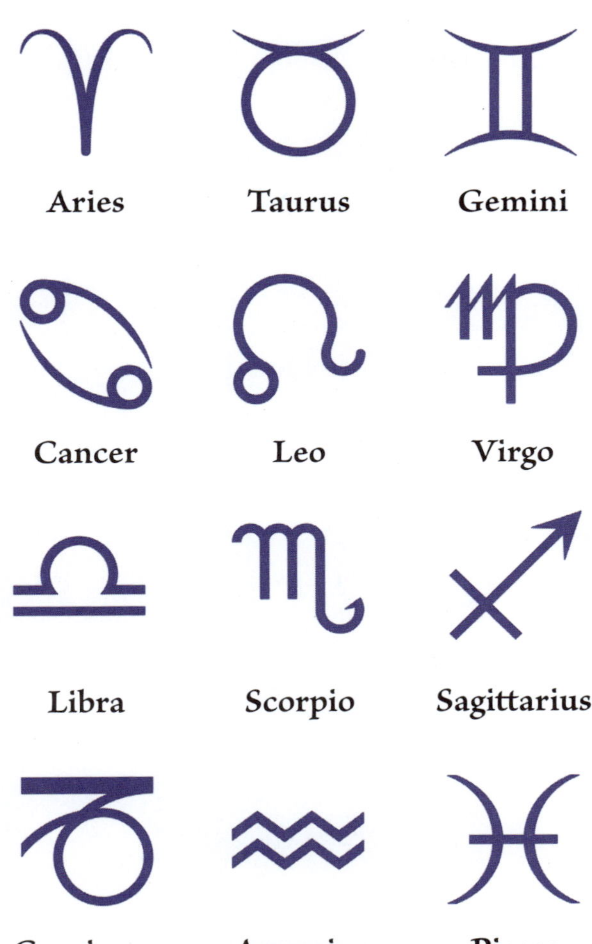

Gemini The Twins

The celestial twins of Gemini are the Greco-Roman semi-divine characters, Castor and Pollux. In recent years, research has demonstrated the amazing similarity between the lives of many twins, even if they were separated at birth. Not only do they share the same mannerisms, likes and dislikes, but they also often make the same life choices, even marrying people with the same names and on the same dates. Then, the same number of years later, they divorce them and marry new spouses, also with the same names! This almost paranormal phenomenon is by no means uncommon, suggesting either that forces other than genes are at work, or that our understanding of the material

carried by genes, and the way they work, is far from complete. Conversely, however, the closest possible type of duos – conjoined twins – can show marked differences in predilections and behaviour. One may smoke while the other hates tobacco, for example. It is, therefore, fortunate that with modern surgical skills as advanced as they are today, it is possible to separate conjoined twins and so, if they survive, give them their own meaningful lives.

In the ancient world, twins were believed to have magical powers, perhaps because of their natural telepathic abilities. The twins Romulus and Remus were believed to have founded ancient Rome in 753 BCE.

The name of the great Meso-American god, Quetzacoatl, means either 'feathered serpent' or 'magnificent twin'.

In ancient Egypt, there were several sets of twins in the pantheon of gods, including Geb, god of the Earth, and Nut, goddess of the Sky, and the more famous Isis and Osiris, with their darker counterparts, Nepthys and Seth.

The duality of twins represented the eternal fight between light and darkness, good and evil.

The Sun in Gemini

Sun sign Geminians tend to be jacks of all trades and masters of none – or at least few. Quick-witted, versatile and adaptable, they love word play and jokes, and are often extremely witty and amusing companions – the life and soul of the party. Expert communicators, they are confident public speakers with enviable timing and panache, and are excellent at networking or bringing shy or diverse people together in social or business situations. The dual sign of the zodiac, Geminians need more than one project on the go at the same time and require constant intellectual and social stimulation. Variety is not just the spice of life, it is life itself for typical Sun sign Geminians, and they can easily become bored and restless – 'twitchy' and nervy if nothing interesting is going on, or if their mind is not being fully engaged. However, even though this is a sign noted for its sharp mind and mental fluency, it can suffer from a very short attention span and lack concentration and stamina. Geminians are inclined to do things in short, sharp bursts and display intense enthusiasm, although a day later they may have completely forgotten that they were even interested in the subject.

Versatile and adaptable, they are quick to turn apparent disadvantages into personal successes, although long-term plans tend to bore them and routine scares them away. As for living alone, it's simply not on the agenda. A Geminian must have an audience or at least someone else to bounce ideas off – and, hopefully, someone who occasionally has the good sense to bring them down to earth with a bump. Gregarious and often actually frightened of being alone, Geminians thrive on constant interaction and

Personality Traits of Geminians

Positive	*Negative*
Quick-witted	Easily become bored and restless
Versatile	Frightened of being alone
Adaptable	Superficial
Confident public speakers	Manipulative
Good networkers	Short attention span
Life and soul of the party	Cold-hearted
Gregarious	Two-faced
Expert communicators	

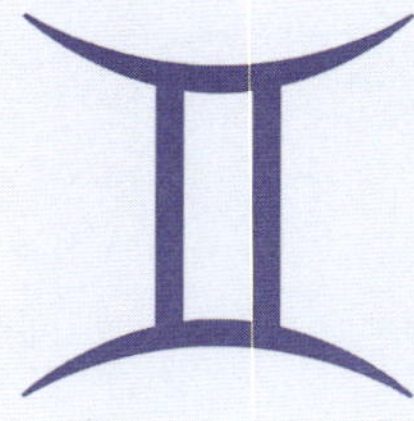

feedback, seeking endless challenges in all areas of their life.

Their major flaws are superficiality and manipulativeness. Ruled by Mercury, their quicksilver minds rarely alight on any one subject long enough to absorb the finer points. They can also be very guileful, sometimes to the point of being accomplished liars and even con artists. The tricksters of the zodiac, Geminians are constantly looking for the main chance, regardless of the cost in human terms. They are frequently cold-hearted and uneasy with the gentler emotions. You will often hear them complain of weariness during major charity campaigns sooner than any other sign of the zodiac. The fact is that Geminians are very uneasy with deep emotions; when faced with strong feelings they tend to take refuge in flippant remarks, sarcasm or logical analysis. Their inconsistency has given rise to the interpretation of the sign of the Twins as being 'two-faced', and there can be an element of truth in that.

Appearance

Wiry and bursting with nervous energy, Geminians tend to be tallish and slim, with indeterminate colour hair, which many of them dye to dramatic effect. When at rest they can appear rather mousey and insignificant, but once they are animated and enthused by life, they light up from inside and can have real star charisma. They have small, narrow hands and feet and quick, sometimes theatrical, gestures. They are Peter Pans, maintaining a youthful appearance to the end, although some of it may eventually come from the surgeon's knife.

Health

Martyrs to nervous prostration, Geminians need to guard against 'burn out' and discipline themselves to get enough sleep and eat regular meals. Because they burn up so much energy, it suits their metabolism to eat a little and often, especially energy-intensive natural foods such as bananas and dried fruit. They are particularly sensitive to the ill-effects of smoking, and should never even consider taking it up – their lungs are delicate and are the first organs to suffer from any debility.

Sun sign Geminians find regular exercise routines a bore, and should maintain a varied programme of sports and martial arts, which will help balance their energies and promote greater powers of concentration.

Career

Although many Geminians are successfully self-employed, they find working alone absolutely unacceptable because they need the motivation and feedback of a workplace – preferably one as busy as possible. The ultimate charmers and communicators, they are particularly suited to media work, especially the ephemeral world of television and advertising copywriting, where their talent for catchphrases can really shine. Fashionable and chic, Geminians are good at creating an impressive image, which allows them to be all the more persuasive when making sales pitches. Indeed, typical Geminians are the salespeople of the zodiac. They enjoy challenges, but feel trapped by deadly routine or too many rules and regulations. A lack of variety can ultimately cause them enormous stress. Many are authors or journalists, often writing two books at the same time or several different articles for a variety of publications. However, don't expect too much depth or an impressive array of facts and figures. Details slow Geminians down: they would rather pay a researcher over the odds than sift their own way through a mountain of reference books. They are often skilled in speed reading and fond of quick fixes, instant answers and immediate responses, which is why they are also naturally computer literate. Surfing the internet is second nature to typical Geminians – once they are online, they can be reluctant to communicate in any other way.

The best careers for Geminians

- Copywriter
- Sales executive
- Communications consultant
- Author
- Journalist
- Television producer
- Tour guide
- Theatre manager
- Actor
- Model

Other suitable jobs for Geminians include tour guiding, parliamentary lobbying, front-of-house theatre managers, theatrical agents, acting, modelling or anything that involves using personality and persuasion. They also make excellent conjurors and illusionists – sleight of hand and sleight of mind being much the same to them.

Unfortunately, Geminians make good career criminals, having the gift of the gab and the ability to lie very convincingly. Many confidence tricksters were born under the sign of the Twins, and even upright Geminian citizens can rarely resist the opportunity to embroider the truth – usually very humorously. Never forget that Geminians can charm the birds down off the trees and then sell them a used car, before persuading them to lie down in the casserole dish and cover themselves with gravy.

Bosses will often be impressed by Gemini energy and initiative, and by their easy assurance and confidence. But their fast talking and often slapdash reports, completed just before the deadline, can cause problems. Geminians find the old-fashioned idea of 'jobs for life' too dreary for words, and often flit from one to another well before they can be shown the door.

Relationships

Geminians who grow up in emotionally undemonstrative families are themselves uneasy with kissing and cuddling, and can actually become distressed by others encroaching on their personal space. But they enjoy being in a lively family and seek partners with strong opinions and marked preferences – at least it's something to discuss and argue over. Talking is always the Geminian's favourite hobby, although listening has to be an acquired skill. They will stay up late into the night talking or strike up conversations with casual acquaintances. Even the normally reserved British have an easy, happy-go-lucky attitude to strangers if they are born under the sign of the Twins. Many

Geminians have relatively few real friends but dozens of acquaintances, and will often insist on bringing them back home for dinner or drinks, or just for a chat, perhaps at an inconvenient time for the rest of the family.

Geminians are keen to make relationships work but tend to be too egocentric and outgoing to ever really know what makes their partners tick, or why they are unhappy. All too often it comes as a terrible shock when they discover the note on the mantelpiece and half the wardrobe emptied of clothes. When they moan, 'Why didn't s/he tell me they were unhappy?' our Geminian honestly has no idea what they did, because they were too busy talking to notice.

Often, Geminians content themselves with playing the field for many years before settling down, being rather proud of their image of being footloose and fancy free. Naturally afraid of commitment or any depth of emotion, the prospect of love for life terrifies them. Others throw themselves into their careers, which they use as an excuse for not having

a partner or even wanting a close relationship. On the other hand, they can be effusively, even sloppily, affectionate with their pets, over whom they can become extremely protective. The uncomplicated loyalty of dogs particularly suits the Geminian temperament, whereas the lofty detachment of cats they can find rather offputting. Traditionally, however, talking birds are the perfect Geminian pets – clever, wily, quick-witted and with a capacity to be funny, although one sometimes suspects it is at your own expense.

Geminians have a multitude of annoying habits, which can add up to major relationship problems. Top of the list is their insistence on dropping everything for some wildcap idea that they have totally failed to think through, and which will end in misery or disaster. And it can be strangely unsettling to try to communicate with someone who does at least three different things at the same time – one of which is always talking on the telephone. (Mobile phones were invented for Geminians.) If you're looking for a nice, reliable partner who is always – literally – there for you, forget your Geminian charmer, who considers being half an hour late to be on time(go instead for a Taurean).

Ideal Partner

Because they often have their head in the clouds, Geminians need a planner, someone who is careful with money. Taureans are too plodding and Capricornians far too pessimistic, but typical Sun sign Virgoans, though they can be

far too analytical and organized, can do the trick if softened with other planetary influences. Perhaps, curiously, it is another air sign – Aquarius – that is ideal for them. Aquarians understand the Geminian restlessness and drive, but add their own gentleness and more profound idealism. Together they make an excellent team, and can even work happily together, either in business or for charity. Geminians need someone who is fairly thick-skinned and independent, someone who can cope with sudden changes of plan, spontaneous outbursts and the chaos that can come with trying to do a multitude of things at the same time.

Compatibility in Relationships

Aries

20 March–19 April

Feisty Arians may seem glamorous, but underneath they are far too serious and self-focused for Geminians.

Cancer

21 June–21 July

Cancerian emotional blackmail and frequent tantrums will send Gemini fleeing. Calmer Crabs might last.

Libra

23 September–22 October

Both real charmers, Geminians and Librans can seem to have something special but they won't be soulmates.

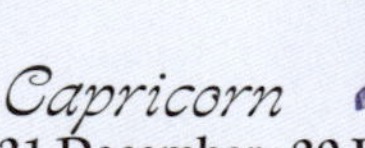

Capricorn

21 December–20 January

The austere Goat may view easy-going and plausible Geminians with suspicion and – justifiable – cynicism.

Taurus

20 April–20 May

Taureans all too often fall for the famous Geminian charm, which will prove too superficial for the heavyweight Bull.

Leo

22 July–22 August

High and mighty Leos can be magnificent lovers but, all too often, there will be a major personality clash.

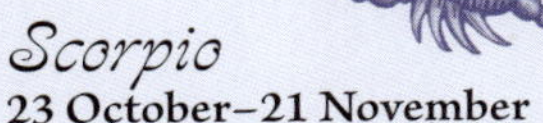

Scorpio
23 October–21 November

Scorpians' glamour will fascinate Geminians and there may be a real sexual buzz, but tears in the end.

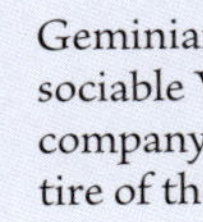

Aquarius
21 January–18 February

Geminians can fall for the challenge of life with a true Aquarian in a big way and find life-long happiness.

Gemini
21 May–20 June

Fellow Geminians know each other's wiles only too well, so this won't usually work for long.

Virgo
23 August–22 September

Geminians can find the more sociable Virgoans good company but they will soon tire of them.

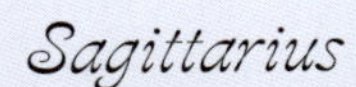

Sagittarius
22 November–20 December

This will be a fun relationship with wild times and big plans, but it won't make for a settled, cosy home.

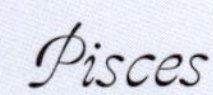

Pisces
19 February–19 March

Geminians have little patience for the often difficult, emotionally intense and rather contradictory Pisceans.

The Geminian Child

Geminians can very easily feel uneasy and out of place, especially when too young to have developed social skills. They need lots of love and encouragement, and need to be given space to be themselves, and to express their energy and creativity. Forever starting a project, hobby or enthusiasm, but rarely staying the course, Geminian children need a firm hand to get anything off the ground. Parents should encourage them to finish off each task before starting the next, although this may be a difficult task. From an early age, they should be introduced to the idea of searching around for information, using libraries and making enquiries so that they learn the value of facts and figures to give their schoolwork some depth. At school and college they will always do better in tutorials and discussion groups than in written work, and they may easily become distracted, more than most, by the drama group or the university magazine. Unsuited to the more ponderous subjects such as philosophy and history, Geminians excel in languages, literature, information technology, media studies and journalism. However, many will drop out in favour of more convivial pastimes, such as becoming stand-up comics or cocktail waiters in fashionable bars.

From an early age, Geminian children should be encouraged to have a great deal of sleep. They career through life at such a breakneck speed that they rapidly use up all their reserves and can become severely run down. They should be made to spend some time winding down before bedtime, to help quell their racing minds and prevent the onset of chronic insomnia. Fresh air and solitude – which they naturally dislike – is necessary for everyone.

Geminian children may not be good sharers or team members, but their capacity for fun and being the life and soul of the party will endear them to most other youngsters, even though they may not make real friends very easily.

Famous Geminians

Bob Dylan

John F. Kennedy

Marilyn Monroe

Isadora Duncan

Prince

Sir Edward Elgar

PC Faberge

Jean-Paul Sartre

Judy Garland

Che Guevara

Marquis de Sade

Anne Frank

Bob Hope

Henry Kissinger

Paul McCartney

Cole Porter

Grigori Rasputin

Bjorn Borg

Al Jolson

Sir Arthur Conan Doyle

Finding Your Sun Sign (2020 dates)

Aries	20 March–19 April*
Taurus	20 April–20 May
Gemini	21 May–20 June
Cancer	21 June–21 July
Leo	22 July–22 August
Virgo	23 August–22 September
Libra	23 September–22 October
Scorpio	23 October–21 November
Sagittarius	22 November–20 December
Capricorn	21 December–20 January
Aquarius	21 January–18 February
Pisces	19 February–19 March

*The dates provided in this book reflect the year 2020.
Dates may vary by a day or two from year to year.